THROUGH THE ANIMALS' EYES

A Story of the First Christmas

Also by Christopher Wormell

Mice, Morals, & Monkey Business: Lively Lessons from Aesop's Fables
The New Alphabet of Animals
Teeth, Tails, & Tentacles: An Animal Counting Book

THROUGH THE ANIMALS' EYES

A Story of the First Christmas
BY CHRISTOPHER WORMELL

RUNNING PRESS
PHILADELPHIA · LONDON

I would like to thank Elizabeth Encarnacion and Frances Soo Ping Chow for their help with this book;

indeed, most of the ideas came from Elizabeth, Frances, and the team at Running Press.

I would also like to thank Elizabeth and Sandra Wallace for their excellent text and Michelle Wescott

for her equally excellent appendix. This book was very much a team effort!

9   8   7   6   5   4   3   2
Digit on the right indicates the number of this printing

Library of Congress Control Number: 2006923190

ISBN-10 0-7624-2669-1
ISBN-13 978-0-7624-2669-0

Cover and interior design by Frances J. Soo Ping Chow
Edited by Elizabeth Encarnacion
Typography: Caslon Antique and ITC Berkeley

This book may be ordered by mail from the publisher.
Please include $2.50 for postage and handling.
But try your bookstore first!

Published by Running Press Kids, an imprint of
Running Press Book Publishers
125 South Twenty-Second Street
Philadelphia, Pennsylvania 19103-4399

Visit us on the web!
www.runningpress.com

For May, Jack, and Peter

LONG AGO, THE EMPEROR DECREED

THAT EVERY MAN SHOULD RETURN TO THE CITY

OF HIS BIRTH TO BE TAXED.

THE JOURNEY TO BETHLEHEM

WAS LONG AND DIFFICULT FOR JOSEPH AND MARY,

AS SHE WOULD SOON GIVE BIRTH.

HER CHILD WOULD BE THE SON OF GOD,

WHOSE KINGDOM WOULD HAVE NO END.

BUT BETHLEHEM'S INNS WERE FULL,

AND HAD NO ROOM FOR THE WEARY TRAVELERS.

SO A HUMBLE MANGER

BECAME BLESSED WITH THE LIGHT OF LIFE.

THAT EVENING, IN THE NEARBY COUNTRYSIDE,

SHEPHERDS WERE WATCHING OVER THEIR FLOCKS.

SUDDENLY,

THE ANGEL OF THE LORD APPEARED BEFORE THEM.

EVEN THE MIGHTIEST TREMBLED.

"FEAR NOT,"

THE ANGEL TOLD THEM, "FOR I BRING YOU GLAD TIDINGS.

A SAVIOR IS BORN, CHRIST THE LORD!"

THE SHEPHERDS HURRIED TO BETHLEHEM

TO FIND THE BABY OF WHICH THE ANGEL SPOKE.

AND WHEN THEY HAD SEEN HIM IN THE MANGER,

THEIR HEARTS WERE FILLED WITH GREAT JOY.

GIVING GLORY TO GOD,

THE SHEPHERDS SPREAD THE NEWS OF

THE CHILD'S GREAT DESTINY.

SOON, THREE WISE MEN FROM FAR IN THE EAST

LEARNED OF THE NEWBORN KING AND

SOUGHT TO WORSHIP HIM.

KING HEROD IN JERUSALEM

LISTENED WITH CONCERN WHEN THESE MAGI

TOLD HIM OF THEIR QUEST.

As the wise men continued their journey,

a bright star guided them to the child in Bethlehem.

THEY SURROUNDED HIM WITH OFFERINGS OF THE FINEST GIFTS:

GOLD, FRANKINCENSE, AND MYRRH.

BUT WHILE THE MAGI REJOICED,

KING HEROD WAS PLOTTING TO DESTROY

THIS THREAT TO HIS POWER.

SO THE WISE MEN, WARNED BY A DREAM

THAT THEY SHOULD AVOID THE TREACHEROUS KING,

TOOK A DIFFERENT PATH HOME.

AND JOSEPH FLED WITH MARY AND THE CHILD
TO EGYPT, BEYOND KING HEROD'S GRASP.

In Egypt they remained, until an Angel told Joseph it was time to bring his family home, where Jesus would fulfill his wondrous destiny.

ABOUT THE ANIMALS

ASIATIC DONKEY: A small, surefooted animal preferred by Hebrews over other packing animals. When families traveled over the rocky, uneven trails of the Holy Land, women and children would ride these animals as the men guided them along.

BLACK STORK: Dark birds with long necks and long orange beaks that eat fish, raise their young near areas of water, and migrate to warmer climates during the fall. Today, thousands of birds migrate to Israel and Eastern Africa in the fall. Among these birds are hundreds of storks that stay in and around the ponds of Israel during the winter months.

GRIFFON VULTURE: A large scavenger bird that builds its nest out of grass and twigs on the cliffs and ledges of mountains. The female lays a single egg, which her lifelong mate helps to care for. The griffon vulture feeds on the remains of dead animals and previously existed in large numbers in Israel. However, it is now struggling to survive against its changing environment, and efforts are being made to increase their numbers.

LION: A large and powerful feline carnivore that was common in the Holy Land during biblical times, but is no longer found in the area. Because of the lion's distinct appearance and its behavior, it has become a symbol for strength, dignity, and courage. In the Bible, the Lion of the tribe of Judah is usually interpreted as representing Jesus.

MOUSE: A small rodent with a furry body and a long, naked tail. Mice have always looked for shelter and food in and around the areas where people live and are considered pests due to the problems they cause.

COW: A large, domesticated beast of burden often used for milk, meat, and labor. During biblical times, cattle were also occasionally used for sacrifices.

CANAAN DOG: A small, domesticated canine trained to contain and protect flocks of sheep and goats from wild animals. Canaan dogs had very strong senses of hearing and smell, which alerted them to intruders both human and animal, even at great distances.

GRAY WOLF: A carnivorous canine that often hunts for its food at night. Wolves frequently stalk vulnerable domestic animals, such as young or weakened sheep in a flock, because of their poor defenses. However, they are easily chased away by humans or dogs.

HARE: A small herbivore with long ears that moves about by hopping rather than walking or running and is usually nocturnal. The hare makes its home in shallow hollows of grass and vegetation called forms. Females line their hollows with their own fur to make a nest for their babies.

DOVE: A small white bird related to pigeons that was frequently found in the Holy Land during biblical times. Known to Christians as a symbol of faith, doves are also often used to represent peace. Doves were believed to contain the spirit of the divine and were present during many important biblical moments, such as the birth of Christ.

ARABIAN ORYX: A grass-eating white antelope with two long horns. The Arabian oryx was hunted to extinction in the wild in the twentieth century, but has since been reintroduced in the area through breeding programs.

SHEEP: A nomadic animal that grazes on field vegetation. Led by shepherds in groups called flocks or mobs, sheep provided wool, leather, milk, and meat for the Hebrew people. In the Bible, Jesus is compared to a lamb when he is sacrificed to save his people.

HIVED HONEYBEE: A small, flying insect identified by the black and yellow stripes on its back. In biblical times, the Holy Land's dry climate and its large variety of flowers were perfect for honeybees. Worker bees use special rhythmic dances to communicate the location of food sources to other bees in the hive.

DROMEDARY CAMEL: A furry, brown beast of burden that can carry people and loads of cargo long distances through the desert. A dromedary camel stores fat in its hump, allowing it to survive for long periods of time without food or water. Its long eyelashes and closing nostrils also offer protection from sandstorms and harsh desert conditions.

ASP: A large, hooded, venomous snake that was also called an Egyptian cobra. Worshipped by the ancient Egyptians, these serpents were commonly used by snake charmers. Despite the theatrics of the snake charmer's musical instrument, the asp's swaying behavior was an instinctual reaction to what it perceived as a threat.

BARN OWL: A nocturnal bird of prey that usually makes its nest in manmade structures such as barns. The barn owl uses its large, quiet wings, sensitive hearing, and excellent night vision to hunt for small rodents, birds, and insects.

GOAT: A nomadic animal that often grazes alongside sheep in a flock. Goats were very important and useful animals in biblical times, providing milk, meat, fur for cloth making, and skin for making water and wine bottles. Similar to sheep, young goats called kids were used in sacrificial ceremonies as offerings against sins.

SPIDER: An eight-leg arachnid that spins sticky, yet beautiful patterned webs to catch the insects on which it feeds. Spiders make their webs by pulling a material called spider silk from their abdomens. Many different types of silk can come from the same spider, and each type of silk has its own purpose in the spider's design of its web. Hundreds of spider species are native to the Holy Land.

EUROPEAN HORNET: A large, flying wasp that is found in Europe, the Middle East, Africa, and North America. Hornets use their stingers to attack prey, such as insects, and to defend themselves and their nests from threats.

LEOPARD: A spotted, feline carnivore once frequently seen in wooded areas throughout the Holy Land, but now rarely found as its environment is shrinking. Leopards are good at climbing and will hang around in a tree to wait for prey walking by.

SYRIAN BROWN BEAR: A large, furry, carnivorous mammal, similar to the brown bear that exists in Europe today. Once commonly encountered in the Holy Land, bears are now rarely seen in the area because of deforestation. In 1932, the Syrian bear was declared extinct in the wild.

EGYPTIAN MAU: A small, domesticated feline that was common in Egypt during biblical times. First used to protect stored food from asps, rodents, and other pests, cats eventually became associated with several Egyptian gods and were revered as sacred animals. However, cats were unfamiliar to most other civilizations, including the Hebrews, during this time.

CHRISTOPHER WORMELL is a leading English wood engraver. Inspired by the works of Thomas Bewick, he took up wood engraving in 1982, and has since illustrated several books in addition to his work in the fields of advertising, design, and editorial illustration.

Long before Christopher became a wood engraver he was taught lino-cutting by his father, mainly for the mass production of Christmas cards. Around Christmastime the Wormell household became something of a cottage industry, with Christopher and his brothers and sisters producing handmade cards by the hundred.

His first book for children, *An Alphabet of Animals*, started as a series of simple, colorful lino-cut illustrations for his son Jack, and eventually grew into a book that took the Graphics Prize at the Bologna International Children's Book Fair in 1991 and spawned a sequel, *The New Alphabet of Animals*. His animal counting book *Teeth, Tails, & Tentacles* was named a *New York Times Book Review* Best Illustrated Children's Book, an American Library Association Notable Book, and a *Kirkus Reviews* 2004 Editor's Choice, among others.

Most recently, Christopher has received acclaim for *Mice, Morals, & Monkey Business*, a collection of Aesop's Fables, which received starred reviews from *Publisher's Weekly, School Library Journal,* and *Kirkus Reviews* and was named an *SLJ* Best Book of 2005. Christopher's other children's book credits include *Mowgli's Brothers, Blue Rabbit and Friends, Blue Rabbit and the Runaway Wheel, Animal Train, Off to the Fair, George and the Dragon, Two Frogs, In the Woods, The Big Ugly Monster and the Little Stone Rabbit,* and *Swan Song,* a collection of poems by J. Patrick Lewis about extinct animals.

He lives in London with his wife and three children.